FIND YOUR
PROPERTY
MANAGER

NOW

hire the right agent and make more money

Jo-Anne Oliveri

Find your property manager now : hire the right agent
and make more money
Jo-Anne Oliveri.

National Library of Australia Cataloguing-in-Publication entry

Author: Oliveri, Jo-Anne, author.

Title: Find your property manager now : hire the right
            agent and make more money / Jo-Anne Oliveri.

ISBN: 9780992385101 (paperback)

Subjects: Real estate management--Australia.

            Real estate investment--Australia.

            Real property--Australia.

            Real estate agents--Australia.

Dewey Number: 332.63240994

Published with assistance by Inhouse Publishing

Table of contents

Find out more about how you can

find your property manager NOW

at ireviloution.com/findyourpropertymanagernow

Introduction

Why this book

If it's broke, fix it. That's my mantra in life. What I've learnt after 20 years' experience as a property manager and property investor is that property managers are property investors' downfall. Investors are not receiving the level of service or financial returns they should be. This needs to be fixed.

During my property management career I have been called many things, good and bad, but troublemaker is one that's stuck. Why? Because if I see a problem then I must solve it. This bothers people because it often requires change. They see it as me simply causing *trouble*. Call it what you like, I say. The fact that property managers are property investors' downfall is a problem I can no longer ignore. It gives the industry a bad name and doesn't fill property investors' pockets. Lose-lose. So here I am once more shaking up the industry and causing trouble.

After so many years working in the industry and investing in property, you could say I've learnt a thing or two about property management and property investment. What makes a good property manager - what makes a good property investor - and the best way they can come together to maximize returns, optimize property growth and build a portfolio.

I know what makes a good property manager after working up the ranks. From property manager and even sales agent to Divisional Manager, Principal and Licensee, Head of Property Management Operations and Development for a franchise group, and finally, Founder and Managing Director of my own company, ireviloution intelligence, which delivers B2B property management services, I learnt that property management success comes down to one key ingredient: education.

Knowing this key ingredient, in my role as Founder and Managing Director I now help make more good property managers. I educate business owners and their property management teams about what is in this book but do so via online training, resources, consulting and other services. Essentially, I make *good* business owners by teaching them how to implement policies and processes to ensure their property managers are molded into good agents –

they deliver the level of service property investors need to make money on their property investment portfolios. Win-win.

Now I would like to help make more *good* property investors because I realized property investment success requires the same key ingredient: education. It's no secret investors are becoming increasingly market-savvy by their own accord. Property managers know this. With easy access to information online – everything from get-rich-quick strategies to property investment hotspots – the answers are out there if you simply ask your web browser. But, I believe there is no information out there like what this book provides. No-one has considered the property investment problem and put forward a solution quite like this book.

Let's get one thing straight though. I don't want you to be disillusioned; this new solution will not make you an overnight millionaire. Just like all things in life, your gain, financial or otherwise, will be relative to what you put in. Don't let that discourage you from reading further though. Once you read this book you'll be an empowered property investor. How? Because this book teaches you a solution to the property investment problem that investors and agents alike may have never considered – how to hire the right property manager.

Right now, property managers may be property investors' downfall but once you, other investors and indeed property managers read this book I hope that will change. If it's broke, fix it. That's my mantra in life. The property management industry needs to be fixed and you are going to help me fix it with this book's solution so you and fellow investors receive a higher level of service and higher financial returns.

The solution

My solution to the property investment problem – that property managers are property investors' downfall – came to me after my experiences as both a property manager and property investor. Namely, my bad experiences in both roles made me realize something was broken. My bad property investor experiences far outweighed the good ones: property manager after property manager brought me frustration and financial loss. Their bad service meant I bore the brunt. I dealt with tenants from hell, personally cleaned my trashed properties and fought my way in court. It wasn't rewarding, financially or otherwise. And, worse still, I knew I wasn't the only one at wits' end with it all. Mingle with any crowd who invest in property and you'll hear your fair share of property manager and property investment horror stories, some of which I'll share in this book. I'm sure you have many of your own too.

But, as an industry insider, I could also see what investors were really up against (why this problem is a problem). Business owners are implementing inefficient policies and processes. How does this affect you, the investor? Inefficient policies and processes mean you receive a second-rate service and don't make the kind of money you want from your portfolio. Policies and processes are how property managers deliver services such as inspections, tenancy renewals and managing arrears. If these are inefficient to begin with then you can forget about those get-rich-quick strategies.

Ready to shake up the industry and cause some more trouble, I asked myself – how can I solve this? For one, I started my own business to teach efficient policies and processes to business owners and their property management teams. And secondly, realizing mine and my friends' horror stories came down to one thing – hiring the wrong agents – I decided to work out how investors could find and hire the right agents.

Who is the right agent? The right agent comes from an agency with proper policies and processes to successfully manage your investment property or portfolio. Such an agent is considered a 'Market Specialist' of your investment property's market area: they have the experience, knowledge and skills to ensure you receive minimal vacancy, maximum returns, the best possible tenant for the longest possible term and optimum capital value. Hiring the right agent puts you in a position to hold them accountable and know that legislation and best practice have been followed in the management of your property and tenants. This is the agent who can make you more money.

But, as you know from your past experiences, property managers turn over like hot cakes. My solution therefore leads you to a representative from the right agency, because it is likely that during your time with one agency you'll see many agents come and go. This is okay because if you hire right to begin with then what remains consistent is the agency itself, specifically its policies and processes as well as your historical data and communication, so your experience should also stay the same should your current agent leave. Your investment property is simply and seamlessly moved on to the new property manager who will also be the right agent as they also represent the right agency.

How can you find this right agent? Ask the right questions. In this book I guide you through a series of questions to ask prospective property managers. These questions separate the right ones from the wrong ones. I know what makes a good property manager, you could say I build these for a living, so trust me, these questions will definitely find you a property manager who can make you more money.

Want proof my solution works? My personal road-test started with a list of agents from agencies in my investment property's market area. I phoned the first listed agent.

"How many properties does your agency currently have under management?" I asked.

The property manager barked down the line, "Why do you want to know that?"

"It's going to help me determine whether I hire you as my property manager."

She didn't like my response, in fact seemed offended and gave me even more attitude (something I'm also trying to stamp out in the industry). Unbeknown to her I crossed her off my list and moved on to the next agent. Agent after agent failed to respond correctly (or at all) to my first few questions despite them being straight-forward. I did have three who managed to answer them and do so correctly, however! I arranged to see these three agents at their respective agencies. When I met with each I asked my remaining questions, namely regarding their agencies' policies and processes and personal careers. None answered all of my remaining questions correctly, but I assumed that would be the case. Nonetheless, I listened to their correct and incorrect answers and at the end of each interview discussed how I preferred certain services to be carried out. One agent listened to my concerns and came to a mutual agreement with me – he would deliver each service how I described. This property manager proved to me that he came from an agency with the right policies and processes. He proved to me that I could hold him accountable. He proved to me that he was the right agent. So, I hired him and have since made more money on my property investment portfolio than ever before. What's more, I am finally enjoying property investment.

Want proof my solution is not a one-hit wonder? I then handed out my list of questions and answers and taught the process to my property investor friends who had one too many horror stories. All friends shared the same success as me. Using my solution they hired the right agents and made more money on their portfolios than ever before. One friend in particular, a scholarly gentleman whose property investment past had almost bankrupted him, came back to me months later and said, "Jo – thank you. Your list of questions has helped me find an agent who has doubled my investment properties' rental returns because she actually understands my market area. I didn't realize such property managers existed!" Well, they do and this book helps you find them.

My tried and tested solution brings you and fellow investors real results. That's because my solution empowers you with the knowledge that's needed to fix the fact that property managers are your downfall. Are you ready to learn my solution? What follows is how you can share the same property investment success that I and countless others have now experienced. I'll teach you the questions you need to ask and answers you need to receive so you find your property manager, now – the right agent who can make you more money on your portfolio than ever before.

Four steps to find your property manager

I'm going to assume you picked up this book because you have purchased an investment property and are looking for a property manager, or you are fed up with your current agent and looking to switch. Either way, you are at the right stage to be reading this book because you are now only four steps away from hiring the right agent and making more money. Essentially, these steps help you uncover facts and figures which tell agencies' stories, good or bad, to lead you to the one you should hire. But, before you get started uncovering these stories, I recommend you read this book from start to finish.

Understanding the questions and answers before you begin working through the four steps ensures the solution works for you and that you find your property manager, very soon.

Step 1: Research

In this step you research your investment property's market area and build your list of prospective agents. You equip yourself with the facts and figures needed to measure and verify agents' answers in the steps that follow.

Step 2: Pre-screen

In this step you send an email (visit our website **ireviloution.com/findyourpropertymanagernow** to download the template) to your list of prospective agents containing the first round of questions. These questions are divided into two areas – agency property management services and market area. The agents you want to take through to the next stage are the ones who correctly answer all pre-screen questions as this means their respective agencies' property management services and market area match you and your property.

Agency property management services questions help you determine an agency's number of properties

under management, management style, ratio of properties to managers, percentage of units and houses,
number of staff, number of years in operation and
average number of years they manage a property.
Agency market area questions help you determine
an agency's market area, management distances,
percentage they manage and average weekly rents.
As well as these questions and their answers, this
book also provides a 'What you need to know' sec-
tion to give you a better understanding of property
management and property investment, and to help
you verify prospective agents' answers.

Step 3: Interview

In this step you conduct a face-to-face or online
video call interview with your short-list of prospective
agents who pass the pre-screen step. The interview
is not a pass-fail mark, however! The interview is
about determining which short-listed agent you
can foresee having the greatest potential for a long-
term mutually beneficial relationship. Interestingly,
this does not mean they necessarily answer every
question correctly. It means you both come to a
mutual agreement about what you want from
the investor-agent relationship. The best way to
determine this is to ask each short-listed prospective
agent every question then evaluate their answers on
a whole. At the end of the interview go back to their

incorrect answers and discuss how you would prefer particular services to be delivered (as outlined in this book). The agent who understands and agrees to what you want is the one you can hold accountable. This agent has proven to you that they come from an agency with the right policies and processes and personally have the right experience, knowledge and skills to manage your property. They have also proven to you that you can hold them accountable. This is the right agent and one you want to take through to the final step – hiring them.

These interview questions are divided into two areas – agency policies and processes and the agent. Agency policies and processes questions help you determine how the prospective agent's agency manages arrears, vacancies, tenancy renewals, rent reviews, maintenance, bonds or security deposits and marketing. Agent questions help you determine how long the prospective agent has worked in the industry and in your investment property's market area. As in the pre-screen stage, under each question and its answer is also 'What you need to know' to give you a better understanding of property management and property investment, and to help you verify prospective agents' answers.

Step 4: Hire the right agent

By this step you have found the right agent and are ready to hire them. Easy!

Hire the right agent and make more money

How do you hire the right agent and make more money? Ask the right questions.

What follows is the research you must undertake, questions you must ask and answers you should receive to find your property manager, now. This is the agent who can maximize returns, optimize property growth and help build your property investment portfolio. This is the agent who can make you more money on your portfolio than ever before. This is the agent you want to hire.

Find Your Property Manager NOW

Step 1: Research

Finding your property manager starts with finding out a few things about your investment property's market area and agencies which service it. In this step you need to find out some facts and figures about your market area and build your list of prospective agents. Why do this? This research helps you measure and verify agents' answers in the steps that follow.

Investment property's market area

The facts and figures you need to know about your investment property's market area are its:

- Average weekly rent
- Average number of days to rent a vacant property
- Average vacancy rate

- Average market growth
- Market demographics
- Average arrears percentage per week
- Bond or Security Deposit Legislation

The easiest way to find these facts and figures is to ask your web browser. Search online for 'Your investment property's country + property investment publication'. This should bring up a list of the leading property investment publications in your country. Click on the first publication search result and look for an area on their website which offers a 'Zip/Post Code Profile', or something along those lines. Type in your investment property's zip or post code and it should bring up a range of up-to-date data on this area. Next, look for the six key statistics you need: average weekly rent, average number of days to rent a vacant property, average vacancy rate, average market growth, market demographics and average arrears percentage per week. Make note of these figures – you'll need them to measure and verify prospective agents' answers in the following steps. If the first publication you click on doesn't offer zip or post code profiles, work your way down the search results until you find one which does.

Likewise, to find out the relevant market area's Bond or Security Deposit Legislation, search your web browser for 'Your investment property's county/

state/territory/province + Residential Tenancies Authority'. Once on the relevant website, search 'Bond Legislation' or 'Security Deposit Legislation' to find out the laws around these subjects. You want to know what must happen at the start of the tenancy when your tenant pays the bond or security deposit, how it must be managed during the tenancy and what must happen at the end of the tenancy. As well as being good legal facts to know if you own investment property, they help you measure and verify prospective agents' answers in Step 3.

Prospective agents list

After you've collected the necessary market area facts and figures, you need to make a list of prospective agents you want to pre-screen and potentially interview. The best way to do this is to search 'Your investment property's zip/post code + state/country + real estate/property management agency'. This gives you a list of agencies located in and near your market area. You only want to deal with agencies located no more than 10 kilometers or approximately six miles from the vicinity of your investment property. The ones which come up in your search should be within this distance, but you may want to check. Once you have verified an agency's location, click through to their website. Websites give great insight into the professionalism of an agency and its agents. Whilst this is quite a subjective assessment, when viewing an agency website ask yourself these questions: Is it set out clearly? Does it look up-to-date (this does not necessarily mean modern, rather, the content is current)? Does it speak to you? If you answer yes to these questions then go to their equivalent of a 'Meet our team' page to note down one of their property managers' names and email addresses, as well as the agency's name. If they don't list their team members and roles, make note of their enquiries email address instead. Soon you should have a list of prospective agents – I recommend between 10 and 20 agents. These are the ones you take through to Step 2: Pre-screen.

Step 2: Pre-screen

As mentioned, in this step you send an email to your list of prospective agents with the first round of questions.

Pre-screen questions

These questions are divided into two areas – agency property management services and market area.

Agency property management services

How many properties does your agency currently have under management?

What is your agency's management style – portfolio or task?

What is your agency's ratio of properties to managers?

What is your agency's percentage of units and houses?

How many property managers and support staff in your agency?

How many years has your agency been operating and what is the average number of years it manages a property?

Agency market area

Which areas does your agency look after and what distance are the managements?

What percentage of the market area does your agency manage?

What are the market area's and agency's average weekly rents?

Pre-screen email

To download the template pre-screen email you can visit our website **ireviloution.com/findyourpropertymanagernow** and click on 'Template pre-screen email'. Once downloaded, copy and paste the contents into a blank email for every prospective agent. Or, to save time, you may like to BCC all prospective agents' emails into one email and paste the pre-screen contents once. Either way, simply fill in the few required details, your investment property's zip or post code and your name, to customize it to your requirements. Once you've done this, hit send! When you receive prospective agents' replies, go through each one and evaluate their answers against the book's answers. The agents you want to take through to the next stage are the ones who correctly answer all pre-screen questions. This means their respective agencies' property management services and market area match you and your property. But, be warned! If an agent has not replied to you within 24 hours this is another sign that their service is not professional. Remove them off your list if 24 hours pass without a reply. Once you have finished evaluating prospective agents' answers you should have your short-list. Don't be worried if, for example, out of the 20 you emailed, only four remain to take through to Step 3. It shows the all-revealing power of these pre-screen questions and means you are even closer to hiring the right agent and making more money.

Here's a copy of the template pre-screen email you can download from our website:

BCC: Prospective agents' email addresses
Subject: Property management inquiry

Hi

I am looking for a property manager to manage my [Insert Zip/Post Code] investment property.

To help me determine whether you are the right property manager for me and my property, could you please answer a few questions about your agency and its market area:

How many properties does your agency currently have under management?

What is your agency's management style – portfolio or task?

What is your agency's ratio of properties to managers?

What is your agency's percentage of units and houses?

How many property managers and support staff in your agency?

How many years has your agency been operating and what is the average number of years it manages a property?

Which areas does your agency look after and what distance are the managements?

What percentage of the market area does your agency manage?

What are the market area's and agency's average weekly rents?

Thank you very much. I look forward to reading your responses soon.

[Your Name]

Pre-screen answers

The pre-screen questions' answers and their background, 'What you need to know', are provided below. Use these to measure and verify prospective agents' answers once you receive their replies from the pre-screen email.

How many properties does your agency currently have under management?

Answer

Find out figure and match to small, medium, large or super agency size – no agency size is necessarily good or bad.

What you need to know

You want an agency which shows growth and retention of business. Such an agency could be small, medium, large or even super-sized because all sizes have their pros and cons. A small agency has around 150 but no more than 200 properties. This agency can provide a high level of specialized service. A medium sized agency has between 200 and 500 properties under management. This agency has an increased market presence due to the high number of properties they advertise. However, once an agency grows beyond 500 properties they usually outgrow their business premises which means you could become a sold off statistic if they are not planning to move their business. A large agency has between 500 and 1000 properties. Such an agency's business strategy could be to grow fast or they could be in the habit of buying rent rolls. However, if the agency has good market presence and dominance, such an agency should never have to buy business. If the agency is growing through business acquisition and not natural growth it usually suggests bad retention of managements. Or, they may be large because they have structured the agency for growth and maintained their high level of service. Finally, there are super-sized agencies – an agency with over 1000 properties. The main advantage with super agencies is their dominance when marketing your property. But, it can also be a curse because your property may be competing against the numerous other properties available through the same agency! Super agencies may have properties spread out across a large distance, which could mean they employ contractors in your property's location to carry out inspections. So, in effect, the super agency is not actually managing your property. Once you find out the number of properties under management you'll know whether it is a small, medium, large or super-sized agency and can then decide if this matches your investment property.

What is your agency's management style – portfolio or task?

Answer

Portfolio-based management.

What you need to know

What's the difference between portfolio and task-based management? One management style makes you money, the other loses you money.

Portfolio-based management means a Portfolio Manager is assigned to you, your property and tenants. The Portfolio Manager's job is to make sure you, your property and tenants are cared for at all times. They manage every process such as maintenance, inspections, marketing, and so on. This is who you need if you want to make more money on your portfolio.

Task-based management means several property managers look after your property. Basically, one agent manages its maintenance, one agent manages its inspections, one agent manage its marketing and so on. This simply decreases your property's potential to make money because information must pass from agent to agent before it finally reaches the agent responsible for carrying out that specific task. Naturally, messages get distorted which often leads to increased disputes, tasks failing to be carried out and you receiving a second-rate service. This style of management also leads to 'pass the buck syndrome' – no one takes responsibility for problems because they blame one of the many other agents managing your property. This is not the agency you want managing your property. Such an agency simply increases your risk of losing money.

There are two tasks where task-based management is okay, however. First, when an agent is tasked to consult with you to select a managing agency. Second, when an agent is tasked to secure a tenant for your property. These two roles are referred to as a Management Consultant and Leasing Consultant. Sometimes, in a small agency, there is one person assigned to both tasks giving them the role of Leasing and Management Consultant.

What is your agency's ratio of properties to managers?

Answer

The agency should have between 170 and 220 properties to every property manager. Each property manager also has an assistant to help manage their individual portfolio.

What you need to know

If the Portfolio Manager is managing between 170 and 220 properties they should also have an assistant, a Property Management Coordinator, taking care of administrative procedures. The Property Management Coordinator is like the Portfolio Manager's apprentice. They help out with administrative tasks of two or three Portfolio Managers. By the time they have finished their 'apprenticeship' and induction into the agency they should have established relationships with clients and team members. In the future, your property may well be assigned to this person. This is good practice. It means the agency's growth is strategically managed. But, if it is a small or start up agency, the Portfolio Manager usually won't have a Property Management Coordinator to help them. This is okay, just be wary of the agency owner's management of their property management division.

What could happen if you hire an agent with no Property Management Coordinator? Before I used my questions to hire an agent, I had a property manager who I had not heard from in awhile. So, I called her and she told me she was too busy managing her 200 properties as she had no assistant helping her. My property manager promised she would inspect my property in the next week. More time passed and, once again, I did not hear from my property manager. I decided to personally check my investment property and found it was clearly not being cared for. So, I decided to review my property's records and found not only had no maintenance been carried out over the past 12 months but the tenant's lease had expired 14 months prior! Property managers managing 170 properties or more need a Property Management Coordinator otherwise you, your property and tenants will not receive the care and attention needed to make you money and you may experience the same horror story as me.

What is your agency's percentage of units and houses?

Answer

You either want an agency with a good balance of both units and houses, or an agency with a percentage that shows they specialize in your style of property. For example, if you own a unit and the agency manages more units than houses, this is a good sign.

What you need to know

This question comes back to what style of property you need managed, usually either a unit or house. If your investment property is a unit you want an agency which manages a high percentage of units.

Such an agency has an extensive knowledge of unit renting and managing in their market area. But, their market area must match your unit's market area for this extensive knowledge to be of use (more on this soon). As an added bonus, an agency which does manage a high percentage of units usually understands how to liaise with Body Corporate and Strata Managers and work with a complex's by-laws on your behalf. Likewise, if your investment property is a house, or similar construction, it is better to hire an agency that manages a high percentage of houses in your property's market area. They should have extensive knowledge on the demographics seeking houses in your market area and specialty processes to manage your style of property.

How many property managers and support staff in your agency?

Answer

If the agency has approximately 200 properties under management you want:

- Two Portfolio Managers
- One Property Management Coordinator (may also act as Agency Receptionist)
- One Financial Controller

Or, if the agency has approximately 500 properties under management you want:

- Three Portfolio Managers
- One to two Property Management Coordinator/s
- One Leasing and Management Consultant
- One Agency Receptionist
- One Financial Controller

What you need to know

You need to understand whether the agency is understaffed, overstaffed or has the right number of property managers and support staff because each influences how much money you can make on your portfolio. An agency with the right number, as outlined above, is financially stable with viable business operations and service standards. Such an agency can make you money. An understaffed or overstaffed agency however, indicates poor operations and poor service standards. Such an agency makes you no or less money than a viable agency. It's that simple.

Unfortunately, overstaffed agencies are the most common. On the rare occasion, an overstaffed agency means they have planned for growth – a good thing. But, more often than not, an agency is overstaffed because of poor (or no) planning. It starts with an agency which doesn't have efficient policies and processes to ensure accountability. This lack of efficiency places increased pressure on property managers and support staff. As a result, tasks are carried out inefficiently, stress levels rise, burnout occurs and more and more staff resign. How does this affect you and how much money you make? High staff turnaround means poor service standards and results in a high turnaround of managements and clients too. Usually what eventually happens to an overstaffed agency is the agency owner continues to employ more and more team members to keep up with the high turnaround. As a result, overheads become unmanageable, the agency runs at a loss and eventually the agency owner closes down or sells up. So, if an agency is overstaffed and not preparing for growth it's best to steer clear of them.

How many years has your agency been operating and what is the average number of years it manages a property?

Answer

There is no right or wrong number of years an agency should have been operating. What matters is that the average number of years the agency manages a property is approximately the same as the number of years it has been operating.

What you need to know

Ideally, you want an agency that has been managing properties for the same number of years it has been operating. This is rare however. So, a more realistic rule of thumb – the higher the number of years in relation to the number of years in operation the better. This shows the agency has good retention, policies and processes and service standards. If the frustration and stress of property ownership is so great that their clients are selling or switching agencies, it is likely this agency is not providing a professional service so will not make you as much money as you would like on your portfolio.

If you want to find out what's really going on, email back asking how many new managements the agency has brought on over the past 12 months. Whatever the figure, subtract it from the number of properties currently under management. This uncovers the truth. For example, if the agency has 150 properties under management and they brought on 10 new managements per month, in 12 months they have 120 new managements. If the agency only has 150 managements now and they have been in operation for several years you have to consider what happened to the other new managements they brought on. You want an agency that demonstrates management longevity. Longevity indicates the agency knows how to maximize returns and optimize property growth, and therefore keep their clients happy.

Which areas does your agency look after and what distance are the managements?

Answer

Your investment property's zip or post code should be one of the zip or post codes the agency looks after. They agency should only manage properties within a 10 kilometer or approximately six mile radius of their agency.

What you need to know

Never deal with an agency that does not specialize in the area where your investment property is located. Why? Because real estate is all about location. An agency must manage a specific location called their 'market area'. You therefore need to hire an agent from an agency located in or in close proximity to your investment property. As a general rule, it should be no than 10 kilometers or approximately six miles from your property.

Now for an insider's secret – in an effort to build business at any cost, an agency may accept managements in locations outside their market area.

This only results in lost income, lower rental returns, lost tenants and excessive wear and tear to your property as the agency's service standards drop with increased travel times.

If an agency does not specialize in the area where your investment property is located then you may find yourself experiencing this next horror story. My property investor friend transferred his investment property to a property manager who convinced him that she could still inspect his property despite it being located in a zip code her agency did not manage. My friend's property was located approximately 20 kilometers away from the agency. However, after 24 months of excuses, lost rent, extended vacancy periods, uncompleted maintenance as the agency's local trades people were unable to travel the long distance, as well as the property manager being unable to show the property due to the long travel time, my friend terminated the management. He learnt the hard way that it did not pay to hire an agent who did not specialize in his investment property's market area.

Another reason to hire an agency located in close proximity to your investment property is because they have local market knowledge. The best possible return and long-term capital growth cannot be achieved if the agency does not have local market knowledge. How can the advice they give you be helpful if it is not specific to where your property is located? If your property is located outside the agency's market area they will most likely struggle to maintain routine or property assessment inspections because of increased travel times, as my friend experienced first-hand. That's because the agent usually puts off your inspections since they are so busy with other tasks. They do not have time to travel the long distance to and from your property. And, once postponed, good luck getting an inspection done until you have tenants moving in or out.

What if your latest investment property is located in a different market area to the rest of your portfolio? My advice, don't use the same agent just because they are managing your other investment properties. There is only one exception – when the agency specializes in executive or prestige rentals. These are niche markets requiring specialized skills. These types of agencies are normally boutique so tend to care for a small but exclusive category of clientele. And, due to their specialized focus, the agency has specialized marketing processes to reach an exclusive demographic – usually businesses, government departments and relocation agencies. So, it would be wise to appoint this same agency if your portfolio's latest addition also falls into the category of executive or prestige despite possibly being located outside the agency's market area.

What you really need to consider in asking this question is does the agency manage any property or do they have a defined market area for which they have specialized market knowledge? The latter is the mark of a professional agency and one you should potentially hire.

What percentage of the market area does your agency manage?

Answer

The higher the percentage the better. However, most agencies' market share percentage is well below 10%. In fact, many struggle to have more than 5% market share.

What you need to know

Most agencies don't know the percentage of rental properties they manage in their market area. Such agencies usually manage a small percentage, well below 10%. That's because many agencies manage properties within a large radius and in numerous market areas. Although such agencies may claim to manage a high percentage of properties, the percentage is actually quite low as many properties are outside the market area's 10 kilometer or six mile radius.

How can you verify their percentage? Use their previous answers. For example, if an agency has 250 properties under management and they manage properties within a 20 kilometer or 13 mile radius, this most likely includes another three or four zip or post codes. If this is the case, you can comfortably half the properties under management. This means they have more like 125 properties within their market area. If there were approximately 8500 properties rented in the location, the agency's market share would be approximately 1.47%. This is a good statistic as it shows they have a small market share. This of course depends on the size of the agency and whether they are a specialist agency however, so take these facts into consideration too.

So, if the agency responds with an overly inflated market share percentage, above 10%, you should then question how much they really know about their market area. Lack of local market knowledge reduces the amount of money you make on your investment property, so beware.

What are the market area's and agency's average weekly rents?

Answer

The market area's average weekly rent should be the same as what your research found. The agency's average weekly rent should be equal to or above the market area's average.

What you need to know

If the prospective agent knows the market area's average weekly rent, they're off to a good start. It shows they are a Market Specialist. If the prospective agent also knows their agency's average weekly rent it is also a good sign they know the area and have proper policies and processes in place. If the agency's average weekly rent is equal to or above the market area's average, this is an even better sign. Something to keep in mind though – if the agency manages properties in various zip or post codes and some of these zip or post codes achieve lower than average market rates for the state, city or territory, this negatively impacts their average weekly rent. However, if this is the case, a good agent also breaks down their market area data into averages for each zip or post code to explain this point to you.

A good agency ensures you receive maximum rental returns on your investment property. They never overinflate the price or under-rent your property as they know both negatively impact you and your property, as well as every other property owner in the market area. Instead, they present you with up-to-date facts and figures to determine the rental value of your investment property in the current market. A bad agency holds back rent increases as they fear they may lose tenants. It is a contradiction if your property manager recommends increasing your rent but suggests you are better off leaving it at its current rate because you may lose your tenant. The tenant would not leave if the rent was at market rate, unless of course they could no longer afford to live in that particular market area.

Hire an agent whose agency holds back rent increases and you may experience the following horror story. My friend's investment property's rent had not been increased for some years, despite good market conditions. His agent advised him the rent should remain the same so they didn't risk losing his tenant. However, the media said rents had increased by an average of 8% in his property's market area. Curious, he asked me to prepare a rental appraisal. I soon discovered the property was under rented by $120 per week. My friend then asked his agent to increase the rent to market rent. But, of course, his tenant could not afford such an increase. Unsurprisingly, his tenant could also no longer afford to rent in the area as the rents has increased so much over the years. His tenant was terminated and his property was advertised. Two days later my friend rented his property for $120 per week more than what he had been receiving. We estimated that in the last two years alone he had lost over $10,000 income because his agent did not increase the rent to market rates. Clearly, you want an agent from an agency which increases rent when necessary, or you may find yourself experiencing my friend's horror story.

Step 3: Interview

Now you have your short-list of prospective agents – the ones who passed the pre-screen step. There is no magic number – it could be all or zero agents who passed. In the rare case all agents fail the pre-screen interview, go back to step one and search online for 'Your investment property's region + investment property style (unit/house) + real estate/ property management agencies'. For example, if your property is a unit and located in Brisbane's Central Business District then you would search 'South East Queensland + unit + real estate/property management agencies'. This should find specialist real estate or property management agencies which may manage an area far greater than your market area but offer specialist skills at managing your style of property. Once you've gathered your list of specialist agencies, put them through the pre-screen process.

Eventually, you'll come away from the pre-screen process with a short-list of prospective agents. These are the agencies who have made it to the next step – the face-to-face or online video call interview. If the interview is face-to-face then it should be at the agency. The only reason you should opt for an online video call interview is if you are not psychically able to get to the agency. For example, you live in New York City and are trying to find an agent for your Orlando property.

Remember, the interview is about determining which short-listed agent in whom you can foresee the greatest potential for a long-term mutually beneficial relationship. It does not mean they necessarily answer every question correctly. It means you both come to a mutual agreement about what you want from the investor-agent relationship. So, ask each short-listed prospective agent every question then evaluate their answers on a whole. At the end of the interview go back to their incorrect answers and discuss how you would prefer particular services to be delivered (as outlined in this book). You may like to first leave the agency to consider their answers and return to discuss incorrect answers at a later time. Or, you may prefer to discuss their incorrect answers immediately following the interview. Either way, the agent who understands and agrees to what you want is the one you can hold accountable. This agent has proven to you that they come from an agency with the right policies and processes and personally have the right experience, knowledge and skills to manage your property. This is the agent you should hire.

Face-to-face/online video call interview questions

These interview questions are divided into two areas – agency policies and processes, and the agent.

Agency policies and processes

What is your agency's average arrears percentage per week and how do you manage arrears?

What is your agency's average vacancy rate and how do you manage vacancy periods?

What does your agency do when the tenant notifies they are vacating?

What is your agency's average number of days to rent a vacant property?

Does your agency recommend periodic or fixed term tenancies?

How does your agency process tenancy renewals?

How does your agency conduct rent reviews and how often do they increase rent?

How often does your agency inspect the property and do you have a copy of the inspection reports?

How does your agency process maintenance?

What happens with the bond or security deposit?

How do you market the property?

Agent

How long have you worked in the property management industry? Tell me about your time in the industry.

How long have you worked in this market area?

Face-to-face/online video call interview answers

The interview questions' answers and their background, 'What you need to know', are provided below. Use these to measure and verify prospective agents' answers provided during the interview.

What is your agency's average arrears percentage per week and how do you manage arrears?

Answer

You want their average arrears percentage per week to be as close as possible to 0% because they have a proactive arrears policy.

What you need to know

The agency's average arrears percentage per week should be 0%. Arrears should never be more than 1%. If they are it shows the agency has a reactive arrears policy, or perhaps no policy at all to manage this process. How can you verify their response? If they give you a general response like 1% they're most likely lying. The correct response should be as specific as 1. 2%. A good agency knows their exact percentage because they are proud of how low it is. Their proactive arrears policy goes something like this: arrears reports are prepared and processed daily by the property manager after rental payments from the previous 24 hours have been downloaded and receipted. Tenants only just in arrears, for example three days but no more, receive an automated message by email or text message. This message is logged on the computer files. This protects the landlord should a claim against landlord insurance be necessary if the tenancy ends in eviction. It also acts as a gentle reminder to the tenant to pay their overdue rent. After five days a further reminder in the same format is sent to the tenant, this time with more urgency for action and warning of the consequences should they fail to pay. Depending on your governing legislation, usually on day seven of arrears and the day before a formal breach notice is issued to the tenant, a phone call is made to warn the tenant of an impending formal breach being issued that will impact their tenancy history. The tenant must understand the consequences of their actions regardless of how good their history has been to date. Despite the tenant's reason for late or non-payment, or if you would prefer to give them the benefit of the doubt, the agent issues the breach notice on the day it can be legally issued. Under most legislation a tenant in a residential property cannot be penalized for late payment of rent. They can be issued with recordable breach notices, however. So, as a property investor, never allow yourself to worry about the possibility of losing your tenant if you issue a breach notice for late or non-payment of rent. Such a proactive arrears policy protects you and makes you more money – it ensures only the best tenants possible rent your investment property.

Hire an agent whose agency has a high arrears percentage, and therefore a reactive arrears management policy, and you may experience the next horror story. My friend phoned me as she was concerned about the amount of arrears she was owed – it was in the thousands of dollars. She could not understand how her agent could allow her tenants to fall so far behind in their payments. When she asked her agent he said the tenants were good people and simply going through a tough financial situation. Meanwhile, my friend was being charged additional interest from the loaning bank for late and non-payment of her mortgage. So, ironically, her agency's lack of arrears policy meant she was now falling into a tough financial situation herself!

What is your agency's average vacancy rate and how do you manage vacancy periods?

Answer

You want their average vacancy rate to be better or in line with the market area's average vacancy rate because they have a proactive leasing policy.

What you need to know

If the agency's average vacancy rate is better or in line with the market area's average it's a good sign they can rent your investment property in the least possible time. How can you verify their response? The agent should know the figure straight away because they are proud of the fact it is in line or higher than the market area's – it shows they are a good agency with a proactive leasing policy in place. If they don't then you could experience longer than average vacancy periods. Take one of my friends' horror stories for example. He received his monthly statement and was shocked to find it had a zero balance. He immediately called his agent to ask why he had received no rent. His agent did not know but said she would get back to him. Unsurprisingly, she never phoned back. A week later he called her again. His agent said his property was still vacant. He was confused – his new tenant was due to move in four weeks prior as his previous tenant had vacated and a new tenant had apparently been secured. However, she then advised him that in the end this prospective tenant decided not to take his property. He then discovered that when this prospective tenant had been approved his property had been removed from the agency's 'For Rent' list. As a result, his property had now been vacant for over five weeks. So, had he not called his agent his property would still be vacant.

A good agency's leasing policy ensures your property is rented in minimal time. That's because a good agency's leasing policy goes like this: a 'For Rent' sign is erected as soon as your property is on the market or when your tenant advises they are vacating at the end of their tenancy agreement. The agency advertises your property online and in other relevant mediums to achieve maximum exposure, only listing your property's suburb, not address. Your property has regular open for inspections. The agency emails enquirers an application form and confirms property details and open times following a conversation with each enquirer. The agent showing your property is skilled at leasing and negotiation. This agent could be the Leasing Consultant in a medium to super-sized agency, Management Consultant in a boutique agency or Property Manager in a smaller agency. The agency has a set process for follow-ups and feedback and not just for you as the owner but for every person who has shown interest in your property. This proactive leasing policy results in your property being leased in the least possible time for the best possible rental rate by the best possible tenant and for the best possible term.

What does your agency do when the tenant notifies they are vacating?

Answer

You want them to have a process for when tenants notify they are vacating. It should be a priority task resulting in your property being advertised within 24 hours of the agency being made aware of your tenant's intention to vacate.

What you need to know

The agency's process for managing tenant notifications for vacating property should go like this: when the agency receives a notification in writing from your tenant indicating their intention to vacate, it should become a priority task. It must be acted upon immediately on the same day of receiving the notification, regardless of when the tenant wishes to actually vacate. If this is not acted upon immediately you may experience the following horror story. My friend's tenant sent a letter to the agent advising they were vacating. However, the agency was closed over the two week Christmas period so the letter was not immediately processed. In fact, due to the huge backlog of work upon the agent's return, the letter was not processed for a further two weeks. In that time, my friend's tenant vacated and her property was not advertised until two weeks later. Having lost a significant amount of potential revenue due to the agency's poor policies and service standards, she terminated and found a new agency which stayed open during the Christmas Holiday period.

In Queensland, Australia, where I live, the tenant has to give the landlord notice to vacate two weeks' prior to the end of their tenancy. On the other hand, the landlord must give a tenant two months' notice prior to the end of their fixed term tenancy (or if the property is sold it is one month's notice). As you can see the property owner is severely disadvantaged in comparison to the notice the tenant has to give in order to leave the property. When two months' notice is given, agencies tend to wait until closer to the time the tenant is vacating before advertising the property. This is poor management. But, the law in most areas allows for a currently rented property to be shown to prospective tenants. A good agency understands these laws and takes them into consideration when writing their agency policy. As soon as a notice to vacate is received, the agency takes advantage of this time and advertises the property. The agency checks the tenancy agreement to ensure the tenancy is almost at the complete term and expires on the date given in the notice. If the tenant is notifying of their intention to leave then the agency has a policy to call the property owner prior to any action being taken to discuss the notice and seek instructions in relation to advertising the property and at what rental rate. The agency provides you with an analysis of available and recently rented properties that are comparable to your investment property. The property should then be advertised and listed for inspection before close of business that same day. A 'For Rent' sign is also erected that same day, or by the very latest,the next day. Once a new tenant is secured, the agency allows three days between tenancies to ensure your property is well and truly ready for the new tenant to take up occupancy. There is nothing worse than

[

a tenant moving in only to find the previous tenant left the property unclean or in bad repair. A good agency always allows for the unexpected.

What is your agency's average number of days to rent a vacant property?

Answer

The agency's average number of days to rent a vacant property should be lower or equal to the market area's average number of days to rent a vacant property. It should not be more than two or three days above the market area's average.

What you need to know

The average number of days to rent a vacant property indicates the length of time from when a property is listed to when a tenant is secured, they have signed up and paid, and the listing is removed from the availability list. If your research in step one shows the market area's average number of days for which a vacant property is listed is six, then this is what you compare the agency's average against. If the agency's figure is even lower than the market area's, this is even better. A figure lower or equal to the market's average shows that the agency has a good leasing policy in place. It means the agency lists a property as soon as the tenant notifies them of their intention to vacate. This minimizes the vacancy period as a new tenant is usually secured within three days of the previous tenant vacating. How can you verify their response? Ask what the market area's average number of days to rent a vacant property is to see if it matches your research. If the agency provides the same figure as your research this shows they are Market Specialists. Such an agency provides market area information, such as this figure, to their clients in the form of reports.

Hire an agent from an agency with a higher than market average number of days to rent a vacant property and you could experience my friend's horror story. Her investment property was vacant for seven weeks. She was told they received no inquiry because the market was slow. After doing some of her own research she found that the average number of days to rent a vacant property was only three days. So, she immediately terminated her agency and listed with another. Her property was then rented in two days and at a higher rent. Clearly, the new agency she hired had a proper leasing policy in place.

Does your agency recommend periodic or fixed term tenancies?

Answer

Only fixed term tenancies.

What you need to know

A good agency recommends fixed term tenancies because periodic term tenancies pose more risks for you as the property owner. A fixed term tenancy means the tenancy has a start and end date. Prior to the expiry of the end date, you and your tenant have the ability to negotiate and secure a renewed fixed term tenancy through the agent acting on your behalf and in accordance with your instructions. It means you can better manage your investment property's financials and know exactly when additional fees are added. On the other hand, a periodic tenancy means there is a start date but no end date. The end date is when you or your tenant provide notice to the other party to finish the tenancy. This makes it difficult to plan for the long-term as at any point and in any market your property might become vacant. This usually results in you being forced to accept a lesser rental rate than before. A good agency would only recommend a periodic tenancy if you are uncertain about what your intentions are with your investment property. For example, you might be considering selling your property in the near future or increasing its rent as soon as possible. With this in mind, and again I refer to legislation in Queensland, Australia, even on a periodic agreement you should provide your tenant with at least two months' notice of your intention to increase the rent. During this time your tenant may decide to vacate the property and legally only needs to give you two weeks' notice. If you wish to evict your tenant, provided it is not as a result of breaches of the tenancy agreement, then you must give them two months' notice in writing. There are also some occasions when a tenant may request a periodic tenancy for a number of reasons, such as they are looking to purchase their own property or soon transferring to another location due to their job. In such cases you may also allow your tenant a periodic tenancy. But beware! If the agency does not charge a tenancy renewal fee, they may not help with negotiations between you and your tenant, such as negotiating a lesser period for a higher rent.

How does the agency process tenancy renewals?

Answer

You want the agency to charge you a tenancy renewal fee and have a process for managing tenancy renewals whereby up-to-date market rental information is provided to you so you can make informed decisions on your investment property's rental rate.

What you need to know

Only deal with an agency that charges a tenancy renewal fee and provides you evidence on how they process, negotiate and manage the tenancy renewal. A good agency charges you a tenancy renewal fee equivalent to approximately one week's rent. This shows the agency places importance on processing, negotiating and managing a tenancy renewal. It is in your best interests to ensure your investment property's tenancy is renewed when it is due as it is your opportunity to ensure your property is earning market rent. It is also your agency's opportunity to review your tenant's behavior and rent paying history to determine if they are honoring their tenancy agreement. A good agency advises if a termination is necessary. A good agency also conducts tenancy renewals in accordance with local legislation by allowing enough time to increase rent where warranted and offering current tenants the opportunity to extend their tenancy term for the best term possible. Or, in the case you instruct the agency to terminate your tenant, the agency sends them the appropriate notices within the required timeframe and ensures they vacate by the last day of their tenancy.

If an agency does not have a proper tenancy renewal process then you may experience this next horror story. My friend's lease agreement was due to be renewed in the next two months. As per the local legislative requirements, the tenant must be given two months' notice to vacate the premises. His agent said they would contact the tenant also as per their policy to see whether they were intending to renew. Predictably, another week passed and my friend didn't hear from his agent. So, he contacted him. His agent told him that his tenant was undecided. Knowing the laws, he requested his tenant be served the vacating document immediately. Reluctantly, his agent served the paperwork. But, upon serving the papers, his tenant advised they were not going to renew. When the agent advised my friend of his tenant's intent, he requested the property be advertised online for rent. This was now six weeks before the property became vacant. Once again the agent advised him their policy was to only advertise properties two weeks before availability. Not happy with this response, my friend instructed his agent to immediately advertise his property. His agent finally agreed and within two weeks they received a suitable application. He accepted the applicant and had a tenant secured four weeks prior to availability. But, if it wasn't for my friend's insistence and knowledge of local legislation his property would have most likely been vacant for far longer.

How does your agency conduct rent reviews and how often do they increase rent?

Answer

The agency conducts rent reviews every six months. Their tenancy agreements have a rent increase clause so you can increase your investment property's rent if there are movements in rates every six months. The agency has a rent review policy to keep up-to-date with market movements and advise you when they occur.

What you need to know

A good agency conducts rent reviews every six months because their tenancy agreements contain a clause setting this out and allowing rental increases if necessary. One exception to the rule may be if there is a special negotiation at the start of the lease, such as the rent may be initially set higher to compensate for upward market movement. Their 12 month or longer tenancy terms also have a special tenancy clause or condition to review and potentially increase the rental amount. When a rental increase is appropriate - due to market movement, a good agency always advises you when to increase rent. They can do this because they spend at least two hours a week researching their market area so they remain specialists of the location and can provide you their findings so you too understand current market movements. The data they provide relates to pending developments or applications for developments, changes and additions to infrastructure, and so on, in your investment property's market area. Ultimately, this cumulative data helps you set or increase rental rates as you can predict market changes based on historical trends.

If you hire an agency which does not conduct any market area research you may not only miss opportunities to increase your rent but you could experience the following (potential) horror story. My friend's rent review occurred during high inflation (4%), increasing mortgage repayments and high rental returns in the market area. His property was returning $600 a week. His agent suggested a $5 (.8%) a week rent increase. When he enquired whether the market would allow a greater increase his agent said it would but advised they did not want to scare his current tenant away. It became apparent that no real research had been conducted prior to the review. So, my friend asked his agent for further research to be conducted. As a result, further research was conducted and my friend came away with an additional $25 (4%) a week increase instead.

How often does your agency inspect the property and do you have a copy of the inspection reports?

Answer

Every 17 or 26 weeks (depending on the market). The agency's property inspections stay in their weekly cycle regardless of tenant movement. The prospective agent presents you with a sample copy of the agency's inspection reports. These reports should be detailed and thorough.

What you need to know

Routine inspections are a major part of the service your agency provides you. A good agency thoroughly inspects your property at the exact frequency and intervals set out in their policy.

Generally, there are differences when it comes to property inspection frequency. Executive and prestige rentals, for example, only need to be inspected every 26 weeks, this is approximately every six months. The recommendation for average rental properties is every 17 weeks, which is approximately every four months. A good agency works on a frequency of weeks rather than months as this guarantees your property is inspected on the same day every 17 weeks and you know in advance when the next property inspection is due. The inspection takes place regardless of the date that a new tenant has taken up residence in your property. For example, if a tenant moves into your property and three weeks later an inspection is due, the inspection is done as scheduled. If the inspection is due 15 weeks after a tenant moves in then that is when the inspection is done. Remember, a tenant who breaches their tenancy agreement should be evicted if the breach is of a serious nature. The only variance is if a public holiday falls on the inspection day. In this instance, the inspection is carried out either side of the public holiday but remains in the same inspection cycle. A good agency also carries out the report using a computer to ensure consistency, regardless of who does the inspection. The report is generated from the previous inspection and the updated with any noted property changes to further guarantee reporting consistency.

Hire an agent whose agency does not have a proper property inspection process and you may get caught in my friend's horror story. His investment property had been managed by the same agency for the last three years. During that time he never received an inspection report. When he contacted his agent she advised him that inspections were being done but she was too busy to send him the reports. He asked for confirmation but confirmation could not be provided. My friend decided to call the agency's business owner to express his concern. The business owner took the property manager's side and told him that if he was not happy to take his property elsewhere. He contacted the Office of Fair Trading to request advice on what to do. As a result, the agency was fined and ordered to refund all management and service fees and commissions to my friend.

How does your agency process maintenance?

Answer

The agency has a maintenance policy. This policy outlines what constitutes emergency and routine maintenance. They have someone rostered to immediately manage emergency maintenance. Routine maintenance is always reported in writing by the tenant, processed daily by the property manager and audited weekly by the agency business owner or team leader.

What you need to know

A good agency has a maintenance policy outlining how and when team members process maintenance requests. They conduct weekly maintenance audits to ensure follow-up, follow-through and completion of every task. That way, if the contractor has failed to gain access, been delayed or is unable to complete the job, at least the job can be escalated or given to a different contractor. They have property managers entirely responsible for managing the maintenance of properties in their respective portfolio. They also teach you and your tenant what maintenance is deemed urgent, emergency or routine. All routine maintenance is submitted in writing to the agency. Unless it is urgent or emergency, the agency does not take any maintenance notifications over the phone as they would be doing you a disservice and placing you and their agency at risk of liability and prosecution. Routine maintenance is processed once per day, not at the time the property manager receives the notification. When an agency does not have a policy of processing routine maintenance that is reported in writing, then the tenant could claim they reported a particular item of maintenance over the phone but the property manager failed to act. A tenant has an obligation under most tenancy agreements to report maintenance when they find it to minimize the potential for it to become worse and more costly for you.

A word of advice – never delay maintenance! Delaying maintenance means it may not only become worse and more costly but you could lose tenants because it is not being rectified in a timely manner. In most countries, the relevant tax law provides an incentive for maintenance whereby its cost is usually a taxable deduction. I suggest you check your own tax rules and regulations to ensure you understand what deductions are claimable through owning an investment property.

Hire an agent whose agency does not enforce a proper maintenance policy and you may experience the following horror story. My friend shared a series of emails with me from her property manager. The first email said her tenant had indicated the dishwasher was tripping the power supply. The property manager requested instruction from my friend about what to do. My flabbergasted friend sent an email back requesting a service person inspect the dishwasher and provide a report about what was tripping it, quote if it needed repair or replacement, or to simply repair it immediately. She could not believe her property manager asked for instructions instead of taking action to minimize her tenant's frustration. Her property manager later contacted her advising that the sound on the recently installed television was not working and she had arranged a technician to check it. My friend asked her property manager if she had asked the tenant what they meant by the sound not working and if they had checked the manual. Her property manager advised they had not. My friend told her agent to cancel the technician and find out more about what the tenant meant. It turned out that when the tenant finally consulted the manual they realized they had accidently changed a setting on the TV.

What happens with the bond or security deposit?

Answer

The agency has a bond or security deposit policy in place which follows the relevant market area's legislative requirements. They only release the bond or security deposit when your investment property is ready for new occupants.

What you need to know

A good agency has a bond or security deposit policy which abides by the relevant legislative requirements. They hold on to the bond or security deposit until the end of a tenancy and under no circumstances use it as a substitute for rent non-payment. The bond or security deposit is simply your safeguard and in-surance requirement, depending on your governing legislation. The agency follows laws relating to the retention of a bond or security deposit and how and where a bond or security deposit should be deposit-ed. If they fail to do so they could be liable for a hefty fine and in some instances face imprisonment. In Queensland, for example, the bond cannot be more than the equivalent of four weeks' rent, unless the weekly rental rate is greater than $700. If the weekly rental rate is greater than $700 then a bond can be negotiated between the parties. The bond must be deposited with the Residential Tenancies Authority of Queensland within 10 days of receipting the money. The bond is lodged together with a Bond Lodgment form that includes details about your property, tenant and signatories. The same signatories, including your agency or simply you if privately rented, must match those on the Bond Refund form when your tenant vacates. The tenant's bond is fully or partially refunded or presented in part or in full to the property owner to cover expenses incurred as a result of the tenant when they vacate. You, your agency and tenant earn no interest on these bonds. All bonds are deposited by the Residential Tenancies Authority into a trust account. By completing the forms when depositing the bonds with the Residential Tenancies Authority, they collate the data such as property address, rental amount, number of bedrooms and style of property. This information is released every quarter. This information provides a wealth of knowledge for both you and the industry to keep abreast of what is happening in your market area. But, as I mentioned earlier, not all locations are the same. This is why it is so important for you to know the legal requirements of your investment property's county, state, territory or province. Likewise, a good agency is one which knows and abides by, via their policy, these relevant bond or security deposit legal requirements.

What could happen if you hire an agency without a proper bond policy? My friend's tenants had just vacated his property. The tenants were renting his prestige property complete with luxury fittings and features. The rent was therefore very high. My friend received reports during his tenants stay about how much they loved and cared for his property. They seemed like 'dream' tenants. His tenants were nearing the end of their six-month tenancy term and advised they would be vacating at the end of their tenancy to return overseas. They wanted their bond refunded immediately as after vacating the property they were going straight to the airport. My friend's property manager felt that as they were first class tenants there would be no problem refunding the bond on their vacate day without first inspecting the property. So, the tenants had their entire bond refunded. When the property manager eventually conducted an inspection, the property was filthy and had sustained thousands of dollars in damage. As it turns out the property manager had never thoroughly inspected my friend's property since when she deemed the kitchen and dining room to still be in good condition she felt no need to inspect further. As a result, my friend was not only out of pocket thousands of dollars in repairs and cleaning, but the tenants' final month's rental payment by check was denied. Their bank account had been closed.

How do you market the property?

Answer

The agency has a marketing policy. They provide evidence of their policy's effectiveness at renting properties. Part of their policy is to tailor marketing to your property's style and zip or post code.

What you need to know

Marketing a property is vital to the success of gaining the highest possible rent for the longest possible term with the best possible tenant in the least possible time. To simply list a property on a popular rental website is not good enough. A good agency has a policy in place which provides you with a marketing plan each time your property is available. This is essential because each time your property becomes available the rental market will most likely be different. The agency also knows the best times to showcase your property. If a property is located on a busy road or highway, for example, a good agent knows it is best showing it during rush hour. That's because many prospective tenants are put off by the fact the property is located on a busy road. Showing such a property at the worst possible time (rush hour) can dispel negative thoughts (e.g. it will be too noisy) by show casing its features (e.g. quiet, as the property has been designed to deflect noise).

Likewise, another property may be best shown in the morning as it attracts families whose children are at school for the day. Every property is different and every property appeals to different demographics. That's why hiring an agency which specializes in your investment property's market area and style is vital.

A good agency also knows marketing is not just about advertising your property. Marketing is about promoting your property to a particular database of prospective tenants, as well as promoting to the agency's sales team who may have clients who cannot find a property to purchase and so opt to temporarily rent. A good agent advises you every step of the way. They let you know what rental rate to set given available comparable properties on the market and how to attract the best possible tenant given current market conditions. They are also experts at writing property descriptions that accurately reflect your property's features and benefits and target the desired demographic to attract maximum inquiry. The agency should also supply you with samples of their past marketing. You can use these samples to determine their level of marketing professionalism.

How long have you worked in the property management industry? Tell me about your time in the industry.

Answer

The prospective agent has worked in the industry for approximately three years, at least. Listen to them chat about their time in the industry to determine if they sound experienced, knowledgeable, skilled and passionate about property management. You don't want an agent who is not passionate about their career as a property manager because their service standards will most likely match their lack of enthusiasm.

What you need to know

Hiring a brand new recruit is not ideal. What's ideal is an agent who has gone through their 'apprenticeship' as a Property Management Coordinator, completed both theoretical and practical training and worked through the ranks to Portfolio Manager. This usually takes approximately three years. The prospective agent must also represent the agency i.e. its' culture, brand, reputation and service standards. You want to uncover the prospective agent's career goals and aspirations to determine their level of property management experience, skill and knowledge. If they are new to the industry, are they supported by an agency which provides training to improve their individual performance and help with career advancement?

How long have you worked in this market area?

Answer

At least two years.

What you need to know

In the same way the agency must have in-depth knowledge of your investment property's market area, the agent you hire must share this same in-depth knowledge – they should be a Market Specialist of your investment property's market area. Obviously, the longer they have been working in the area the more knowledgeable they will be. So, rule of thumb, the longer they have worked in the area the better it is for you. Even if they are relatively new to this particular agency, their previous agency may have managed properties in the same location. Their knowledge should be about the market area's past, present and future. This information should be based upon facts, statistics and demographics. The agent should provide you information regarding the demographics looking for your particular style of property, what those potential tenants are seeking in a property, the recommended rental rate and how your property will stand out from other properties currently available in this area. An agent who knows your investment property's market area provides rental market appraisals based on the current supply and demand. They also provide you with a list of truly comparable properties, not just properties with the same number of rooms. This is a simple task for agents who are Market Specialists. And the longer the property manager has worked in the area, the bigger their database of comparable properties. They also know what is happening in the area, in terms of development and plans for new infrastructure. Development and infrastructure impacts your property both in the short and long term. Ultimately, you need to hire an agent with this local market knowledge for your own short and long term planning.

Hire an agent who is not a Market Specialist and you may experience the next horror story. My friend was upset when she terminated the management of her property because her favorite property manager transferred to another agency. She felt confident with the way this agent had managed her property. So, this favorite agent of hers reassured her that even though he was not working in the area he could still care for her property as he knew its history. However, several months after transferring, my friend noticed things weren't being done. She soon realized that her property manager was not keeping up with what was happening in her property's market area so, as a result, she lost valuable income and her property was not cared for. Her favorite property manager was now no longer a Market Specialist of her property's market area and, unfortunately, my friend paid for it big time.

Find Your Property Manager NOW

Step 4: Hire the right agent

Are you feeling empowered? You should be. Property managers need no longer be your downfall when it comes to property investing; you now know how to hire the right agent and make more money on your property investment portfolio than ever before. With this knowledge you and fellow investors can receive the level of service you need to make higher financial returns and, finally, enjoy property investing!

As you now know, the way to fix the property management industry is through education. I hope you agree this is the key ingredient for property management and property investment success alike. Knowledgeable property managers and knowledgeable property investors know how to work together to maximize returns, optimize property growth and help build your property investment portfolio. This book has taught you the questions you need to ask and answers you need to receive to ensure you are a knowledgeable property investor and hire an agent who is, likewise, knowledgeable.

Once you reach this final step and have within your grasp the agent who has proved to be the right one, your days of property investment horror stories are over. To complete the process of finding your property manager, you must simply hire this right agent and hold them accountable to what you both agreed on. Out of the prospective agents you interviewed, consider which one not only answered most questions correctly but then listened to your concerns and came to a mutual agreement on how services will be delivered. If you find that perhaps a few of your short-listed prospective agents meet this criteria then my advice is to go with your gut – which one feels right. Who can you truly foresee having the longest and most mutually beneficial and financially rewarding relationship with? This is the one you should hire.

So, you have reached the end of the book. If this is your first time reading it I recommend you put it aside for awhile and consider what I have taught you. Once you feel you understand the process and what is involved, it's time for you to find that right agent. Begin the four steps to find your property manager and you will find the one who can maximize returns, optimize property growth and help you build your portfolio. This is the agent you want to hire. And this book helps you find them, now.

Find Your Property Manager NOW

Final thought

One final word of advice before you begin the four-step process. To further help you find your property manager, we've put together an online resources library you can access by visiting **ireviloution.com/findyourpropertymanagernow**. As well as the template pre-screen email, you'll find more information about property management and property investment to help empower you as a property investor.

On that note, I sincerely hope this book and its additional resources lead you to long-term property investment success – good luck!

Notes

_____

_____

_____

_____

_____

_____

_____

_____

_____

_____

_____

_____

_____

_____

_____

_____

_____

_____

_____

_____

_____

_____

_____

_____

_____

_____

_____

Find Your Property Manager NOW

_____

_____

_____

_____

_____

_____

_____

_____

_____

_____

_____

_____

_____

_____

_____

_____

_____

_____

_____

_____

_____

_____

_____

_____

_____

_____

_____

_____

_____

_____

_____

_____

_____

_____

_____

_____

_____

_____

_____

_____

_____

Find Your Property Manager NOW

_____

_____

_____

_____

_____

_____

_____

_____

_____

_____

_____

_____

_____

_____

Find Your Property Manager NOW

_____

_____

_____

_____

_____

_____

_____

_____

_____

_____

_____

_____

_____

_____

Find Your Property Manager NOW

Find Your Property Manager NOW

_____

_____

_____

_____

_____

_____

_____

_____

_____

_____

_____

_____

_____

Find Your Property Manager NOW

www.ingramcontent.com/pod-product-compliance
Lightning Source LLC
Chambersburg PA
CBHW071521200326
41519CB00019B/6029